Tragedy, Ecstasy, Doom, and so on

Tragedy, Ecstasy, Doom, and so on

Poems by

Kip Knott

Cover design: Kip Knott and Julie Zaveloff
Cover art: "After Rothko's 'Rust and Blue'" by Kip Knott

ISBN: 978-1-952326-18-9

Kelsay Books
502 South 1040 East, A-119
American Fork, Utah, 84003

For Dana and Callum. Thank you for not giving up on me.

Acknowledgments

The following publications were kind enough to publish selections from this book, sometimes in earlier versions:

Journals/Magazines:

2River View: "In Memoriam" (published as "Voices")
The American Journal of Poetry: "The Twelve Stations of Mark Rothko," "Strange Bedfellow," "21st Century Vesper," and "Tonight I Drink Alone"
Barrow Street: "Institutional" and "Van Gogh's Cloud"
Cathexis Northwest Press: "Dylan and Cash Sing 'Girl from the North Country'"
Cream City Review: "Creation Myth" (published as "Hide and Seek")
The Ekphrastic Review: "Seven Sadnesses"
Flights: "The Half-Life of Echoes" (published as "Expanding Echoes") and "Self-Portrait with a Smile"
Four and Twenty: "Vanishing Point"
The Gettysburg Review: "Insomnia"
La Piccioletta Barca: "Before the Morning Begins"
Lullwater Review: "New Year's Eve" (published as "At the End of the Century")
Mudark: "The Seven Dreams of a Mythical American King"
One Sentence Poems: "Temporary Agnostic"
Poems & Plays: "Salvador Dali's Typical Nightmare"
Right Hand Pointing: "Encoded"
Spring Street: "Sequential"
Typishly: "A Walk after the Evening News"
Virginia Quarterly Review: "Doldrums"

Chapbooks:

Whisper Gallery (*Mudlark*, 2004): "Askew" and "Life in a Cloud House"
Everyday Elegies (Pudding House, 2007): "The Distributive Property of Multiplication over Addition," "Existential Sociology," "Self-portrait in a Broken Mirror," "Speculative Autobiography," and "Traveling Salesman"
Afraid of Heaven (Mudlark, 2013): "Afraid of Heaven," "Bigfoot Crossing," "The Night Word," "One Day," "The Politics of Hurricanes," and "Tools"

Anthology:

I'll Be You When You Get There: Poets Write to Their 17-year old Selves (Black Air Press, 2019): "Boxes"

Contents

I. The Biography of Fire

Creation Myth	15
Existential Sociology	16
Note to a Drowned Poet	17
The Distributive Property of Multiplication over Addition	18
One Day	19
The Night Word	20
One Sunday	21
New Year's Eve	22
Insomnia	23
A Walk after the Evening News	24
Askew	25
Self-Portrait in a Broken Mirror	26
Self-Portrait with a Smile	27
Van Gogh's Cloud	28
Institutional	29
The Seven Dreams of a Mythical American King	30
Dreaming without Falling	33
Salvador Dali's Typical Nightmare	34
Traveling Salesman	35
Speculative Autobiography	36
Sequential	37
Vanishing Point	38

II. Rothko's Gospels

The Twelve Stations of Mark Rothko	41
Seven Sadnesses	53

III. Every Day Takes

Every Day Takes   61
The Half-Life of Echoes   62
In Memoriam   63
Forgone   64
Strange Bedfellow   65
Tools   66
21st Century Vesper   67
The Politics of Hurricanes   68
Dylan and Cash Sing "Girl from the North
    Country"   70
Bigfoot Crossing   71
Afraid of Heaven   73
Tonight I Drink Alone   74
Doldrums   75
Encoded   76
Boxes   77
Before the Morning Begins   78
Meditations at the Town Dump   79
Temporary Agnostic   80
When My Son Asks if There Is Anything Left in
    This World to Bring People Together   81
Breaking Home Ties   83

I'm not interested in the relationship of color or form or anything else. I'm interested only in expressing basic human emotions: tragedy, ecstasy, doom, and so on.

—Mark Rothko

I.

The Biography of Fire

Creation Myth

When I sleep I slip into a hollow oak to hide
from a child who counts against an ash.

Outside my new door the world moves:
stones snail over dirt, roots step out

of the earth, branches gather fallen leaves.
The child breezes past calling deep

into the woods. I lean back and wait,
the cool pulp of rot kissing my neck.

The longer I stay, the tighter the tree
holds me. Slowly my skin turns

dry and hard as woodpeckers jitter
up my spine. My hair grows into

every branch and my arms break through
deadwood, pink leaves blossoming

from my fingernails. A starling builds
a nest in my mouth. The woods call my name.

Existential Sociology

after James Galvin

A large black
overcoat falls off a coat tree
and it is the end of the universe.

An old man grabs for it,
which brings us to the end.

A dove flutters inside the pocket
like a magician's forgotten trick.

We all die

and the song the birds always sing
comes to an end,

the song about the old woman
who crawls into the ground

while digging in her garden.

Purgatory of flame, sulfurous nights,
the moon knows what time it is
and where it will sleep.

Keep weeping.

In the song it rained salt
and we all died of thirst.
Off the coat tree

a large black overcoat falls
and no one picks it up.

Note to a Drowned Poet

We haven't learned a thing, Li Po.
The plum trees outside
government buildings are fruitless
and dwarfed.
Street lights do the rest,
irradiating the night clean of stars and dark.
Every vagrant wears a yellow halo,
and when one leans over filthy water
to wash his face,
he drowns in the reflection
of a man-made moon.

The Distributive Property of Multiplication over Addition

Some days we regret
the sun emptying the sky
of darkness and stars.

Some days we regret our parents,
their morality, their religion,
their rules, their discipline,

their hands, their genes.
Some days we regret
our husbands or wives.

Some days even our children
cause us to pause,
reassess, reevaluate, regret.

Multiply one regret
with another regret,
and the result is always zero.

And so the question becomes:
Is zero as empty
as the hole at its center?

And so we are left to answer:
Even the emptiest days are full
of regrets.

One Day

It is the day too far off
to be considered real.

It is the day fathers promise sons
whenever they ask for something
that cannot be given.

It is the day to hope for,
the day all prayers will be answered.

It is the inevitable day
that blindly follows orders.

It is the day I sent two letters to:
the first inviting it to hurry up;
the second begging it to take its time.

When or whether ever
those letters will arrive,
God only knows.

All that I know for certain
is that today is the only day
that isn't tomorrow
or yesterday.

The Night Word

is a curse word
that burns like stars
in a dark throat
damning you for another
forgettable day,

is a broken word
whose splinters imbed
in your fingers
when you try to piece them
back together,

is a holy word
that absolves you
of the sins you are bound to
commit beneath a blind
and blacked-out new moon,

is the last word
that defines the whole
of your life
the way smoke writes
the biography of fire.

One Sunday

I used to count myself among the sinners. I would
join them every Sunday in a cave-like cathedral

and chant demands for absolution
like a sleeper cell waiting for the word.

Once activated, we would rise up and strike down
any unsuspecting enemy with our testimony.

Secretly, though, each of us was ready to sell out
the other for the simple promise of salvation.

In the end, it only took one Sunday to accept
that Sunday was just another day of the week,

one Sunday when I awoke to the sound
of a lone Junco, its beak battered and bloody,

attacking its own reflection in my bedroom window.

New Year's Eve

No night is ever small or celebrated
without consequence, like the last night of the century.
(In Times Square everyone is in a hurry
for the ball to fall.) Tonight, a finger of moonlight
rattles my keyhole. Owls build belfries
under my window, their barks a strange tolling.
Unable to sleep with all the bleating, horses
let the lambs out of the gates then roust the cattle.
Moths give a broken alarm clock to the bat.
And all through the night, homeless mothers
throw dolls of presidents into graves that hold
the wicks of their starved children.

I will find my own way when I wake,
and cook my own breakfast, and open the letter
I wrote to myself when I was a boy.
Dying stars ring out above my head
for the world to hear should it choose to listen.
The rising sun lights the fence of trees
lining the horizon. Under my pillow, only a hole
where the night lay like a pulled tooth.
I don't know who sent the invitation to suffer,
but for now, on behalf of no one, please accept it gladly.

Insomnia

Turn your back on me tonight. Don't let me see
your red opossum eyes staring back from the dark.
My pillow is my other child: I hold him to my chest
when I dream of things forbidden I have in common
with every other man I'm tied to on this earth.

I'm warning you, the bed hums with electricity.
Don't come too close when you slide your body next to mine:
one touch is all it will take to wipe your brain clean of memories.
And we have so many, you and I. How many nights
have we made love in my La-Z-Boy at 2 a.m.

while my wife walks alone in a dark field of white poppies?
Remember our first anniversary? The toast we drank?
One sip of scotch for our first night together; another sip
for all the nights ahead of us; a final sip for your child,
the son who pulls me nightly from the deep well of sleep.

So many memories can't be worth losing
for the sake of a night awake with me. So many
memories that if you were to stack one atop the other
like all the pills I've swallowed in vain to keep you away,
they would stretch at least to the sun, that great disk

of sleeplessness you honor with my every waking hour.

A Walk after the Evening News

The whole world seems off
kilter. Even birds overhead
fly at jagged diagonals, suturing
the sky until the sun warms
only the backs of clouds.

Around me, the papery skins
of birch trees sluff off
in long strips about my feet,
exposing bare and vulnerable trunks.

Carved into the face
of one lightning-dead sycamore,
someone's name gapes
as if trying to shout
Hello! or *Goodbye!* or *Help!*
I quickly move on before
the lightning that struck it strikes me.

I slump on a log to get my bearings,
but the world descends upon me
like notes in a minor key,
disconnecting me from myself
until I am a silent drone
untethered, alone,
spying on the man I used to be,
the man who always knew
his way back home.

Askew

The other man that I am
when I dream sleeps alone.

He dreams of the other man
he becomes when he sleeps,

perhaps of me lying here tonight
too many dreams apart from him.

Self-Portrait in a Broken Mirror

A stranger stares back from the mirror as I shave.
Looking deep into his eyes, I wonder
if he is just as surprised to see me
as I am surprised to see him,
if the timing of his heartbeat matches mine,
if he remembers the profound and mundane
details of his life as I remember mine.

Does he remember the lunar eclipse
his mother woke him to see so he would know
how the dark can become darker?

Can he still see the flag-draped casket
of his P.O.W. pen-pal roll across
the TV screen on the evening news?

Can he still feel how his skin burned
the first time his father showed him how to shave?

Does he understand how
each new pair of shoes has led him
inevitably to where he now stands
staring at a face with a hundred smiles
as sharp as the shards of the mirror he broke
one morning when he didn't recognize his own face?

Self-Portrait with a Smile

Let me begin with a simile
as complex as the coordination of muscles
it takes to create a smile
so as to divert your attention away
from the scars that smile across my wrists.

No. That's a lie. I have no smiles
on my wrists, no reason to divert your attention
away from anything about me.

Do you see the white spaces here between each stanza?

If you look deep into those caves,
you might find what I'm really hiding.

Or maybe the narrow channels between
the lines hold more than silences.

The real trick is to speak
these words aloud and really listen.
Then you might hear what I'm talking about,
but only if you close your eyes
and quit looking for a smile that isn't there.

Van Gogh's Cloud

Heaven is a gaudy mansion.
A chandelier of stars someone forgot to turn off

illuminates its massive foyer.
A dim corridor connects rooms labeled

Chagall Blue, Klimt Gold, Beckmann Red.
Van Gogh opens the door to the yellow room,

a room of sunflowers and wheat.
The air is heavy and damp, unbreathed.

The scent of gunpowder fills
the empty spaces he leaves in his wake.

Institutional

Van Gogh smokes a pipe in a locked room
      with no electricity,
            his ghostly face a blank canvas of white,
the pale field where irises will bloom
      against against each other.
            His hollow eyes stare out into a light,
the bright world of Arles where blackbirds loom
      over ripe and windblown wheat.
            I stare back from a world of locks, of trite
artists brimming with gloom and doom
      and clichéd thoughts of suicide.
            The man next door knows Kurt Cobain was right:
a shotgun blast sanctifies the tomb
      for the mourners left behind.
            The anorexic girl upstairs is slight;
she shuffles like a possessed broom
      over linoleum floors,
            recites Sexton from memory, a rite
performed when pills rattle down the flume
      of her dry and bony throat—
            I have gone out, a possessed witch—a flight,
an escape from her windowless room
      and forced feedings before bed.
            I, however, look to Van Gogh for sight,
look deep into his eyes for the plume
      of madness that consumed him.
            I am a smoking wick, a small white light
glowing where purple irises bloom.

The Seven Dreams of a Mythical American King

I saw the rich giving workers either
gold or silver or rice,
but when they asked for their own reward,
no one was left.
　　　　　—"The Message of King Sakis"

Night One

I dream suspended in a cage of talons.
Below pass vast grasslands,
a brown river that tears the land
in two, then mountains
and deserts and mountains again,
and, just out of my grasp, the tops of trees
only God could have planted.
One day the walls of my kingdom
will touch two oceans.

Night Two

Over an open ocean,
a great bird drops me
for a fish that could feed my people
an entire winter. I fall
through cold salt water and land
in an open oyster. In time,
my skin turns smooth and opalescent
until I become more pearl than man.
When I wake, I know that Hell
is not the oyster but the pearl
inside—God, man, and devil born
out of the irritation of a grain of sand.

Night Three

Naked, I wander the woods
for a safe place to sleep.
The world is kind and gives
me an abandoned snail shell.
Inside, spirals curl into white distances.
Outside, a cloud hangs
from the moon like a threadbare coat.
I labor through corridors of grass,
hefting my home on my back.

Night Four

I've had this dream before,
I know. The boy who wanders
the woods blindly calls
from a hollow chestnut tree.
When I look inside, the pulp
crawls with bagworms.
I decree from this moment on
that all houses in my kingdom
must be built of stone.

Night Five

A dozen black wolves
sniff my motionless body.
The wolf with yellow eyes
drags me by my hair
deep into her lair
where two albino pups suckle

from her swollen breasts.
When I wake, I tell my soldiers
to load their guns.

Night Six

In this dream I am loved
and feared for my golden touch.
Throughout my long life
my subjects keep their distance.
They have learned the consequences
of my caress. But they have also learned
how to harvest endless wealth from death.
Alone, I try to write my lonely story,
but the pages become too heavy to turn.

Night Seven

I see my body ablaze,
but there is no apotheosis.
Rather, all of my people stoke
the flames and dance
in the strange light of my dying.
When my last ember cools,
they feed my ashes
to the goats and pigs.
Nothing of me must survive.

Dreaming without Falling

In 1930, Alvin "Shipwreck" Kelly broke his own record
by sitting on top of a 225-foot tall flagpole for 49 days.

How long, really, is 49 days? Long enough
to breathe in and blow out enough breaths
to call that time a life lived? Depending on one's perspective,
49 days can pass as fast as the blink of an eye
or seem to last as long as the time it takes to count
the number of blinks one blinks in 49 days.
How did Shipwreck Kelly measure his 49 days atop that pole?

The first 23 days may have been the most difficult,
a kind of Hellish déjà vu with nothing new to excite him,
simply a repeat of the feat he had completed one year before
fueled by gallons of black coffee and an endless chain of smokes.
And yet, even after day 24 he stayed perched like a grotesque
above Atlantic City, breaking his own new record 25 times over,
perhaps afraid of living a grounded life that added up to nothing.

Like Christ in the desert, he must have confronted temptation
daily: the craving for one morsel of solid food that,
for reasons of decorum, life atop a flagpole did not permit;
the chance to carry on a quiet, intimate conversation with anyone;
and most of all and all the time, the desire for warmth—
the warmth of his toddler son filling his arms and chest,
and the electric heat of his wife's body next to him in bed.

Unlike Christ, though, there was nowhere for him to wander;
one moment's lapse in concentration meant certain death,
a literal fall from grace. So on night 48, he made sure to
slip his fingers once again into holes he'd drilled into the pole
and lash his ankles to the tiny platform he called home to prevent
his dreams from becoming one last falling nightmare to jolt him
awake, wild-eyed and breathless, before he hit the ground.

Salvador Dali's Typical Nightmare

He sits at a green and white Formica table
tucked in the breakfast nook of a blue stucco split level.

He scoops wedges of pink grapefruit
out of a mottled rind and flips through the morning paper

propped on a tea pot in front of him. He reads the stats
of yesterday's Giant's/Saint's grudge match

while a woman dressed in a purple terry cloth robe
scrambles two brown eggs in a Silverstone skillet.

Because he is on a post-Christmas diet, he sprinkles
a pink packet of Sweet-N-Low on a few slices of grapefruit.

He licks his neatly trimmed mustache for the last drops of juice,
belches quietly, adjusts his paisley necktie, straightens his hair,

kisses the woman in the purple terry cloth robe,
walks out the front door, and gets behind the wheel

of his two-tone brown Oldsmobile Cutlass Cruiser wagon.
The freeway crawls with the usual rush hour traffic.

He hums "A Rose in Spanish Harlem" as it plays on the radio.
In less than thirty minutes he'll be behind his desk.

When he wakes, his fingers tap at the air as if punching the keys
of some machine, trying to remember how the numbers added up.

Traveling Salesman

I keep all the pieces of my life piecemeal
rather than pieced together as something whole
so that all the ghosts I own won't go mad.

As it is, they hang content as empty slips
on velvet hangers deep in a closet
so cluttered I'm afraid to open the door.

Consequently, I'm forced to travel light anymore,
like a man who wears only the smell of his skin
and invites the world to breathe him in.

I wander here and there without a sales pitch.
People pass and never look back;
any one of them may carry the final piece.

But without a shirt to cover my flesh,
I have no sleeve on which to pin a bleeding heart.

Speculative Autobiography

I spend the day speculating
about my life, at least
the last days that walk toward me
as fast as I walk toward them.

Histories aren't supposed to be
personal, but the two men
who pass on the crosswalk
know each other for themselves.

They look surprised
by the recognition they see
in each other's eyes.
One knows he must kill the other.

What he doesn't know is when
and how. A rock to the head?
A quick shot to the chest?
Simply doing nothing at all?

The irony is God-like. Together,
the two men move straight ahead
in opposite directions,
circling inevitably back

to this moment, to this crosswalk,
each waiting on opposite sides
of the same street
for the lights to change.

Sequential

The pen, the pad, the dog on my lap,
the end-table, the newspaper, the steaming cup of coffee,

the empty couch, the clock marking the empty minutes,

the branch tapping windowpanes speckled with rain,
the indecisive weathervane squeaking on the roof,

the dispossessed headlights streaking down the road,
the driver, lost but not lost, heading straight for home.

Vanishing Point

I have finally reached the inevitable
clearing in the woods, that place
where looking down the path behind me
and looking up the path that lies ahead
is the same as looking into my grave.

From nowhere in particular
and everywhere around me, dispossessed
voices whisper stories of my life
I was too young to remember
and stories I have not yet lived to forget.

II.

Rothko's Gospels

The Twelve Stations of Mark Rothko

I. *Rothko Chapel*

A gate—just a gate—
half-opened
(or is it half-closed?)
filled only with air
(or is it absence?)

disturbed by

the last person
who passed through
either departing
or arriving
home.

II. *Self-Portrait,* 1936

You have constructed yourself
as if you were nothing more
than rough-cut blocks of sandstone
and granite, cold and geometric.

Your body stands like a Roman
column, a place to hang angle iron
arms capped with mallet hands
and rest your finial head.

Your face, bespectacled and brutal,
is neither a window nor a mirror.
Your face is a void,
a place consumed either by
a blinding light or a blinding darkness.

III. *Entrance to Subway,* 1938

Even this early the blocks
of color you built your life upon
are there. But so are people,

shadowy apparitions penned in

between columns preventing
the world above from claiming

their two-dimensional world.

The only way out is down,
where something unseen lures
faceless travelers, lures us, below

into incandescence.

IV. *Hierarchical Birds,* 1944

The only parts of them that fly
are heads liberated from bodies

by the razor's edge of the horizon
that separates the sky—mottled
purple and blue like a new bruise—
from the sandy-tan earth
entombing their flightless carcasses.

The war has plucked them clean
until they are less than birds
and more like exclamation points

anchored to the canvas,
exclamation points
screaming rather than singing.

V. *Rust and Blue,* 1953

An ocean between two darknesses:

one darkness plum-like,
the darkness that arises
from somewhere deep within
the earth after sunset
and fills with stars;

the other darkness coagulated
as old blood spilled
from a suicide's wrists.

You want us to swim
across that ocean,

but you refuse to tell us
which direction we should to go.

VI. *Purple, White, and Red,* 1953

Three supine bodies
hover
diaphanously

like ghosts of the colors
they claim to be
and perhaps once were,

or apparitions of long departed
loved ones, present and yet
not entirely whole,

or prayers spoken so often
their words, unburdened
from all meaning, float

from the lips of the faithful
and diffuse into nothing

before ever reaching Heaven.

VII. *Black in Deep Red,* 1957

It could simply be night
descending

or the morning
sun rising.

It could also be
the apocalypse blooming

in some vast desert
where men ravage

the empty spaces
that separate them

from their God.

VIII. *White Cloud over Purple,* 1957

Look closely and you will see
the anatomy of an A-bomb blast:

the pregnant belly of the fireball
bulging like an over-ripe orange;

the layer of radioactivity
luminous as an opal;

the ghostly shockwave enveloping
everything in a silken shroud.

IX. *Red on Maroon,* 1959

It's not a well,
although it runs deep
and is not bottomless.

It's not a window,
although looking into it
means looking out.

It's not a door, locked
or otherwise, nor is it
a foundation holding nothing.

It's not a cataracted eye,
or a mouth forming a muted cry,
or a corrupted mind.

It's not one thing or another,
although whatever you make of it
in your own mind

becomes everything,
becomes nothing,
becomes you.

X. *Horizontals, White over Darks,* 1961

It is not a brooding cloud
hovering over your world
of stacked caskets,
but it is a cloud nevertheless,

brighter toward the center,
frayed at the edges
as if shredded by weather
or unsettled thoughts.

And yet, as one darkness
blurs into another darkness,
as blackness fades from gray
into the brown of earth,

the light, though not heavenly,
becomes a transitory oasis.

XI. *Orange, Red, Yellow,* 1961

You stack flames
one atop
the other like so much cordwood.

No. Not cordwood.
More like bodies
piled on a pyre:

the top body thin and freshly dead;
the middle body just beginning to inflate;
the bottom body bloatedly old.

All of them
together
feed your silent conflagration.

XII. *Black on Gray,* 1969/1970

At the end, a tarnished silver
straight razor sliced the painting in half,

its precise line demarcating

the honed edge on which you lived
from the shadow that called you home.

Seven Sadnesses

You've got sadness in you, I've got sadness in me—and my works of art are places where the two sadnesses can meet . . .

—Mark Rothko

I. *Underground Fantasy,* 1940

Did you see the people in this painting as iron bars
of some hellish cell of your own making?

Did you believe that if you kept stretching them
they would break free of your canvas prison?

Did you see everyone around you
as nothing more than unstruck matchsticks?

Did you conjure these wick-thin
underworld wraiths from nightmares?

How could you know in 1940
what the dead of Buchenwald would look like?

II. *Untitled,* 1948

After the war destroyed the human form,
your paintings began to transform
into some new lifeform

conjured from your own imagination.
As Creator, you could have titled this painting
"Zygote" or "Embryo" or "Fetus."

"Overture" could have worked, too,
which suggests something
bolder yet to come.

As you grew older, you may have surrendered
to the palette and designated the painting
"Blue over Orange and Yellow."

By the end of your life,
you may have only been able to assign
a number, maybe "3."

But in the way that you made
the multiform colors reach toward
one another as if trying—but failing—

to touch, to connect, to combine,
perhaps the best title is
no title at all.

III. *Yellow, Blue, Orange,* 1955

You attempt to suppress
your darkness beneath
a block of sunlight
that is both bright

and waning.

You attempt to leach out
all traces of despair
and leave a cool lake
whose waters, you hope,

will calm your fevered mind.

IV. *Four Darks in Red,* 1958

You have created a world
where gravity is unchained.

What was once darkest and heaviest now floats
unrefrained above

an incandescent landscape
illuminated by a wholly unnatural light.

V. Rothko's Dinner at the Four Seasons, Autumn 1959

It was meant to be nothing more
than a scouting expedition
for a prospective new commission,
an opportunity to examine the space
where unsuspecting patrons
would guzzle champagne
surrounded by the portals
of your monolithic paintings.
There was no better place,
you believed, to wage war
against a class of people
who needed to face the abstract
reality of a damaged world.

You slowly scanned the swanky room
formulating a plan of attack:
your paintings—your weapons—
would hang low, no higher
than five feet from the floor,

so that their detonations would devour
everyone, consume the consumers,
deposit their remains into some private void
only to be reconstituted back
into something close to human.
You saw this as your last chance
to become God-like, to become Creator,
Destroyer, and Redeemer.

But with each new bombastic course
(Caviar on Ice, followed by
Watercress Vichyssoise, followed by
Lobster Thermidor, followed by…
followed by…followed by…)
your appetite waned
and your resolve disintegrated.

When they ignited the Crêpes Suzette,
you stood suddenly, your immaculate
white serviette falling silently
to the floor like a flag of surrender.
Staring into the dancing blue flames,
you realized for the first time that winning
this war meant sacrificing yourself
to the ravages of friendly fire.

VI. *Black on Maroon*, 1959

A banner of blood
stretched, decomposing,
necrotic at the edges:

your sigil for a world
undyingly loyal
to suffering.

VII. *No. 4,* 1964

Even you knew that sometimes
there is safety in numbers.

Even you, having lived so long
moving from one dark space to another,

you who made a habit of inhabiting emptiness,

you who saw your paintings
not as windows but as mirrors,

you who buoyed yourself on the back of blackness

the way a dying star relies on the night
to prove that it still has some light to give,

even you found those moments
when you could not—or would not—
name the darkness.

III.

Every Day Takes

Every Day Takes

one more memory
as your synapses snap off
like faulty fuses. There goes the image
of your son, his first wobbling steps
taken across the family room
(or was it the backyard?)
before he fell into your anxious arms.

Your wife's middle name, the spelling
of which you once corrected
when she got it wrong
while renewing her driver's license,
dissolves letter by letter
into perfect, blinding whiteness.

You try to preserve each endangered
memory as if it's a firefly you can pin
to corkboard and label for future reference,
but the Rosetta Stone of your mind
can't even decipher the hieroglyphs of scars
you've carried with you all your life.

Every day takes—. Every day takes—.
Every day takes you one step closer toward
the absolute purity that is the blank space,

that is the blank space
of your life stretching out into infinity.

The Half-Life of Echoes

There are memories that never leave this world.
There are caves where these memories echo

for millennia, unheard until a shepherd
searching for his lost flock stumbles in.

The shepherd tilts his head toward the whispers
he's unsure he's heard or simply imagined.

He calls out "I am here!" and waits for a reply.
Fear whispers into his ear, and he turns and runs

back toward the light that tethers him to his life,
leaving behind the tiny fossils of his words.

In Memoriam

In these woods,
elms drunk on rain
step out of their bark
and cry for you.

Are you hiding in the light
of invisible animals?
A blue jay cackles
as if it knows.

The steady voice of an oil well asks
Where? Where?

In the distance, the brittle Ohio
breaks and the throats
of smokestacks choke on stars.
Darkness blossoms in bare trees.

Your memories echo
from the white cave
of this page.

Forgone

Memory is the wolf that takes the shape
of absence wandering like a snowdrift
in the wind. His tracks are never empty.

He knows his way when you are lost. The stars
call to him, but the moon is his master,
marking months and years in quarters and halves.

Listen: His stories are your stories, too.
Look for him when the new moon steals across
the sky; follow his path without question.

Soon enough you won't remember a thing.

Strange Bedfellow

Each night when you lose yourself
behind unsettled lids, a stranger finds you,
asks you your name,
where you've come from,
where you're heading.

You politely answer each question:
You know me.
I'm from you.
I'm going wherever you're going.
Now let me ask . . . .

But before you can finish your question,
the stranger turns and walks away.

You step into the hole he leaves
in the air where he stood
and fill his place in the world,

unsure of who you will be
when you climb out of bed in the morning.

Tools

The cellar is full of them, cobwebbed
together like unused synapses.

Every morning I take inventory. Every morning
something new goes missing, the outlines
of handsaws, planers, and pliers on the peg board
filled with nothing but holes.

I shine a flickering flashlight into
dank corners, rummage through crumbling
boxes with labels too faded to read.

But what's gone missing stays missing.

Maybe they were never there at all,
like early childhood memories planted
in my brain by shadowy photographs.

Or maybe the only tool I really need
is a spirit level to even out all the aspirations
in my life that have gone sideways.

21st Century Vesper

Reduce the world to its minimum:
two dimensions rather than three.
Fold the mountain in the distance
like a piece of paper and slip it in your pocket
alongside the shadow that you carry
with you, a handkerchief you can take out
to cover your face when you weep.

In your new two-dimensional world,
prayers are too voluminous to exist.
At first you attempt to compensate for the loss
by trying to resuscitate the flat clouds
that stick to the sky like Colorforms.
Eventually, though, you learn to love
the absolute primary brightness of the world.

And as the parallax of years scrolls past,
all such prayers fade like the colors
in a long forgotten coloring book
along with all your memories of the Gods
who compelled you to stay within the lines.

The Politics of Hurricanes

In elementary school I was made to learn
the lives of saints and patriarchs
so I would know the triumph and meaning of suffering.
I can still see Sister Mary Alonzo's eyes well
as she described—arms raised to Heaven—the angel
who saved a bound Isaac from his father's blade.
And when my father raised his belt to punish me
for some minor sin or other, I prayed
for that same angel to come and save me.

I was also made to watch stuttering filmstrips
of Sputnik orbiting Earth like an all-seeing eye
and grainy movies of atomic explosions so I would believe
my teachers when they told me to duck and cover.
As I watched, horrified, a radioactive storm obliterate
a house just like my own in one Godly superheated breath,
I came to accept the terrible truths before my eyes:
Strong wind and Satan were one and the same,
and one day we would all pay for our collective sins.

And when my father explained that thunder was God
clearing his throat before damning Commies
with His tongue of lightning, I took every word as gospel.
Each night, my father by my side, I prayed for God
to keep me safe from the Red monster under my bed.
Once tucked in and left alone, I whispered my own pray
to beg off the storms in my dreams. But as I grew older,
no prayer could keep them away. Each new storm blossomed
into a hurricane named for every one of my sins:
Envy, Sloth, Gluttony, Greed, Lust.

Even now I dream of hurricanes, their whipping
winds stripping the flesh from my bones
and scattering my remains everywhere and nowhere

as if I were nothing more than a Challenger astronaut.
But tonight, as I watch satellite images of a new hurricane
tighten around an empty, devilish eye
surrounded by lashes of rain bands curling over Florida,
I can't help but pray for the angel to free Isaac
once more so that he may strengthen and grow
and scrub the world clean of acrimony, hate, and God.

Dylan and Cash Sing "Girl from the North Country"

The Johnny Cash Show, June 7, 1969

If I had been riding a train through Nashville
that day, I would have begged the engineer to hush
the profane chatter of clattering steel wheels
so everyone could hear Bob's country-nasal
twang as it rang out through the windows
of the Ryman Auditorium like rain
hammering a tin roof in sunshine. One verse in,
Johnny's booming voice blew through the lyrics
like a dust-devil roaring over hardscrabble,
a wind strong enough to knock down
the walls that separated Americans

from Americans. And when their voices sang
together, they echoed a growing thunder;
not the deafening, bone-rattling thunder-
clap of Apollo 11 that would shake the world
little more than one month later,
but the burning summer thunder that rumbled
down the back of my father's throat
at the end of another long day
of carpet bombings, lottery drawings,
casualty lists, and bloody protests on TV
when one shot of whiskey turned into two or three.

Bigfoot Crossing

When I was a kid, I believed
wholeheartedly in Jesus and Bigfoot.

I tasted Jesus in the bread I ate every Sunday,
which satisfied my faith in Him

and in my father's assurances
that all my sins could be washed away

as long as I never stopped believing
bread was not bread but flesh.

I wanted my father to believe with me
that Bigfoot was real, too,

not a man in a gorilla suit but a missing link.
I had the proof hanging on the wall

over my bed like an icon in the form
of the "Bigfoot Crossing" sign

park rangers posted on a road
curling up the side of Pike's Peak.

But I doubt my father ever noticed anything
on the few occasions he entered my room—

not the crucifix with the hidden Holy Water
compartment above my dresser,

or the Lincoln Log cabin I had built
to remind me of my dreams

of living off the land like Grizzly Adams
in some cloister of the Rocky Mountains,

or the G.I. Joe P.O.W. camp laid out
meticulously on the floor of my closet,

complete with tortured U.S. soldiers
missing fingers on their Kung Fu grip hands.

If I was lucky, he entered my room beltless
simply to give me his pair of scuffed penny loafers

to shine so I would know before I fell asleep
what it meant to walk a day in his shoes.

Afraid of Heaven

I promised not to tell my father on his deathbed
that I believe angels are dead things,

that I've only seen them in the dark
wells of my dreams, their white faces smiling

like bleached skulls shining in full moonlight.

Tonight I Drink Alone

Because the sun rises every day
     only to fall on its head and forget.

Because stars forget to sheathe their talons
     and shred the dark to light.

Because night forgets that crows are nothing
     but feathery shards of itself.

Because gravestones over time forget
     the names of those sleeping beneath them.

Because the new moon forgets to shine
     and stares down upon me

like a bottomless black eye.

Doldrums

In the stillness of a windless day,
trees stand full, and proud, and straight.

But you see in the windlessness
the inevitability of your life's last day

when your breath will be the final small gust
of air to stir the leaves

that shade your face from the indifferent sun,
the day when you realize you haven't lived

the life you thought you would hack to pieces
and burn like so much firewood.

Encoded

The last thing you see when you drift to sleep
is yourself watching yourself drift to sleep.

Every day your life folds into itself
until one day you will be forced to embrace your own death.

Inside your chest, the man you will become when you die
spends his days tapping out an encoded message

you cannot ignore but choose not to decipher.

Boxes

When the time comes to open the cardboard box you keep
under your bed, you will find inside an old pine box.
Inside the pine box you will find a yellowed ivory box,
then a silver box, then gold. With each new box

your excitement will grow less containable.
After six boxes you will begin to curse Hungarian curses
your grandmother taught you when you were just a boy.
Eventually, you will come to the last box,

a stone box too small to open with your hands
stiff and gnarled from a lifetime of hard work and worry.
You will try jimmying the lid with your pocket knife,
beating the box with a hammer, stomping on it,

cracking it open in your vice like the walnuts you husk,
running it over with your well-traveled car,
but nothing will work. Exhausted, you will give up,
flip on the TV, plop on the couch for a nap, and dream

of the treasures you locked away too many years ago to remember,
as close as your irregular heartbeat, as distant as the nearest star.

Before the Morning Begins

To remind myself who I am
every morning, I look in the mirror.

This morning I see only
the reflection of the window at first,

its daisy-patterned curtain billowing
toward me, then sucked back and away.

Nothing about the curtain suggests it's alive,
but it breathes nevertheless,

inhaling and exhaling the same air
that fills my weathered lungs.

But when I look deeper into the mirror,
I find my face, pale and bleary-eyed,

wrapped in a gaudy shroud of flowers.

Meditations at the Town Dump

I look out over the dump's fetid pond
where an abandoned dinner table
drifts like a birch bark canoe.

Slick rainbows of creosote
and kerosene ripple out from an oily
bubble bloated like a bullfrog's throat.

I fling a rippled hubcap and shatter
an empty forty, releasing a white froth
that floats over gray water.

I imagine drowning, tugging
at green and blue wine bottles
bobbing over my head for sips of air.

A waterstrider whisks past, weaving
fine, momentary webs. The table lists.
What wants free of me is leaving.

Temporary Agnostic

For a moment I believed
in the possibility of something
beyond this life

as I watched my son roll
down the hill past
familial headstones,

the tiny bones of dandelions
clinging to his hair.

When My Son Asks if There Is Anything Left in This World to Bring People Together

I tell him
everyone lives under the same sky,
and, like all of us, the sky has many faces—
light and dark and shades falling
somewhere in between those two absolutes.

I tell him
the sky whispers its history
in wisps of shifting breezes;
wheezes for help when nooses
of factory smoke wrap around its throat;
howls objections in hurricanes and tornadoes;
cries out in thunderclaps
when lightning strikes a whip across
a back already scarred with vapor trails.

I tell him
always to remember
our sky is not ours alone,
but the place where his breath and mine
join too many other breaths to count:
sea breaths and mountain breaths;
the breaths of six Kingdoms;
breaths propelled by passion
and breaths huffed out in hatred;
first breaths and last breaths.

      I tell him
it is true that the same breath that gives
love its shape breathes life into hate.

      But I also tell him
it is true that a single breath pollinated
by many other breaths blooms into one
all-encompassing atmosphere breathed in
by him, breathed in by me, breathed in
by everyone under one sky, the same sky.

Breaking Home Ties

for my son off to college

For 18 years I've gathered stray feathers
together like bouquets plucked
from the air, tiny trophies to the wind.

I've stitched them back together into wings
with glistening sutures of blood
my heart has no room left to hold.

When I blow on them as I once blew on your face
to wrinkle your nose before you could walk,
the stone in my throat cuts my breath short.

Even now, spread out as if ready to fly,
the feathers feel weightless
in my palms, like handfuls of dandelion fluff.

And yet, at this moment, I am unable to lift
my arms to embrace you when we say goodbye.

About the Author

Kip Knott's writing has appeared in numerous journals and magazines in the U.S. and England, including *The American Journal of Poetry, Barrow Street, Beloit Fiction Journal, Gettysburg Review, Long Poem, Poems & Plays, The Sun,* and *Virginia Quarterly Review.* He has received grants from the Ohio Arts Council in both poetry and playwriting and is also the author of four poetry chapbooks: *The Weight of Smoke* (Bottom Dog Press); *Whisper Gallery* (Mudlark); *Everyday Elegies* (Pudding House); and *Afraid of Heaven* (Mudlark). Currently, he teaches literature and composition at Columbus State Community College in Columbus, Ohio. In his spare time, he is an art dealer who travels the Midwest and Appalachia in search of those lost treasures that can still be discovered at small town flea markets and antique stores. To access more of his writing, go to www.kipknott.com.